The Funny Zone

CLASSROOM ZONE

Read Jokes. Write Jokes.

Jokes, Riddles, Tongue Twisters & "Daffynitions"

By Gary Chmielewski

Illustrated by Jim Caputo

A Note to Caregivers and Educators:

As the old saying goes, "Laughter is the best medicine." It's true for reading as well. Kids naturally love humor, so why not look to their interests to get them motivated to read? The Funny Zone series features books that include jokes, riddles, word plays, and tongue twisters – all of which are sure to delight your young reader.

We invite you to share this book with your child, taking turns to read aloud to one another, practicing timing, emphasis, and expression. You and your child can deliver the jokes in a natural voice, or have fun creating character voices and exaggerating funny words. Be sure to pause often to make sure your child understands the jokes. Talk about what you are reading and use this opportunity to explore new vocabulary words and ideas. Reading aloud can help your child build confidence in reading.

Along with being fun and motivating, humorous text involves higher order thinking skills that support comprehension. Jokes, riddles, and word plays require us to explore the creative use of language, develop word and sound recognition, and expand vocabulary.

At the end of the book are activities to help your child develop writing skills. These activities tap your child's creativity by exploring numerous types of humor.

Above all, the most important part of the reading experience is to have fun and enjoy it!

Sincerely,

Shannon Cannon

Shannon Cannon, Ph.D.
Literacy Consultant

NORWOOD HOUSE PRESS

P.O. Box 316598, Chicago, Illinois 60631
For information regarding Norwood House Press, please visit our website at:
www.norwoodhousepress.com or call 866-565-2900.

Designer: Design Lab

Paperback ISBN: 978-1-60357-680-2
The Library of Congress has cataloged the original hardcover edition with the following call number: 2007035267

Printed in Guangzhou, Guangdong, China.
251N—032014
0214/CA21302438

STUDENTS

Jackie came home from her first day at school.
Kari asked her: "What did you learn today?"
Jackie replied: "Not enough, I have to go back tomorrow!"

Madison: "Let's play school."
Joseph: "Well, OK. But let's pretend I'm absent."

Maria: "Olivia, how do you like school?"
Olivia: "Closed!"

James: "Teacher, there's only one pair of boots in the coat room and they're not mine."
Teacher: "Are you sure?"
James: "Yes! Mine had snow on them."

Teacher to the noisy class: "Order! Order!"

Jeffrey: "I'll have spaghetti and meatballs."

Why do students have such good eyesight?
They're *pupils*!

Why did Emma bake her term paper?
The teacher said she wanted it well done!

Teacher: "Sandy, why are you standing on your head?"

Sandy: "I'm just turning things over in my mind!"

Teacher: "That's quite a cough you have, Tim. What are you taking for it?"

Tim: "I don't know. How much will you give me?"

Teacher: "Kevin, how old were you on your last birthday?"

Kevin: "Seven."

Teacher: "How old will you be on your next birthday?"

Kevin: "Nine."

Teacher: "That's impossible."

Kevin: "No it isn't. Today's my birthday and I'm eight!"

4

I thought a thought.

But the thought I thought wasn't the thought I thought I thought.

If the thought I thought I thought had been the thought I thought,

I wouldn't have thought so much.

Teacher: "Dwayne, I think you have your shoes on the wrong feet."

Dwayne: "No I don't—these are the only feet I have!"

5

Teacher: "Cassandra, what would you do if a man-eating tiger was chasing you?"

Cassandra: "Nothing. I'm a girl!"

George: "Today, I gave my teacher something she will never forget."

Kim: "An apple?"

George: "No. A right answer!"

Were the test questions hard?
No, the questions were easy. It was the answers that were hard!

Teacher: "Tamika, I said to draw a cow eating some grass but you've only drawn the cow!"

Tamika: "The cow ate the grass!"

Where do children grow?

In a kindergarten!

Why should a school not be near a chicken farm?

So the pupils won't hear any *fowl* language!

What school do you go to to learn to greet people?

Hi school.

What animal runs around the classroom stealing answers?

A *cheetah*.

TEACHERS

A tutor who tooted a flute
tried to tutor two tooters to toot.

Said the two to the tutor, "Is it harder
to toot or to tutor two tooters to toot?"

Why were the teacher's eyes crossed?

She couldn't control her pupils!

Teacher: "Class, we will have only half a day of school this morning."

Class: "Yea! Yea!"

Teacher: "We will have the other half this afternoon!"

When should teachers wear dark sunglasses?

When they have bright students!

LUNCH TIME

SQUARE ROOT
Diced carrots

Dad: "Kevin, why on earth would you swallow the money I gave to you?"

Kevin: "You said it was my lunch money!"

9

MATH CLASS

MULTIPLIERS
Tools you need in math

AN ADDER
The kind of snake that knows his numbers

Math teacher: "If I cut a steak into two parts, what would I get?"

Lupita: "Halves."

Teacher: "Right, and then cut in half again?"

Lupita: "Quarters."

Teacher: "Right, and again?"

Lupita: "Eighths."

Teacher: "Right, and again?"

Lupita: "Hamburger!"

MULTIPLICATION TABLE
The longest piece of furniture in the school

Math teacher: "Clyde, if you put your hand in your right pocket and found $1, and then put your hand in your left pocket and found $1.25, what would you have?"

Clyde: "Someone else's pants!"

What did one math book say to another math book?

"Boy, do I have problems."

Teacher: "If 1+1=2 and 2+2=4, what is 4+4?"

James: "That's not fair! You answer the easy ones and leave us with the hard one!"

Teacher: "Now class, whatever I ask, I want you all to answer at once. How much is six plus four?"

Class: "At once!"

Teacher: "Kathryn, why are you doing your math sums on the floor?"

Kathryn: "You told me to do them without tables!"

Teacher: "Tom, are you good at arithmetic?"

Tom: "Well, yes and no."

Teacher: "What do you mean, yes and no?"

Tom: "Yes, I'm no good at arithmetic!" .

SCIENCE CLASS

Why didn't the skeleton pass the test?

He didn't have any brains.

Teacher: "Can anyone tell me what a shamrock is?"

Lauren: "It's a fake diamond!"

Teacher: "Can anyone give me the name of a liquid that won't freeze?"

Emily: "Hot water."

Teacher: "George, how can you prove the earth is round?"

George: "I can't. Besides, I never said it was!"

Have you read any mysteries lately?

I'm reading one now.

What's it called?

My science book.

Christy: "Is it true that the law of gravity keeps us on this earth?"

Teacher: "Yes."

Christy: "What did we do before the law was passed?"

Science teacher: "David, can you tell me one substance that conducts electricity?"

David: "Why, er . . ."

Teacher: "Correct, David—wire."

Teacher: "Ava, what is the outside of a tree called?"

Ava: "I don't know."

Teacher: "Bark, Ava, bark!"

Ava: "Bow, wow, wow!"

Teacher: "Chris, an electric train is traveling south and the wind is blowing east. Which way is the smoke going?"

Chris: "There is no smoke, it's an electric train!"

Science teacher: "Sandy, do you remember the chemical formula for water?"

Sandy: "H-I-J-K-L-M-N-O."

Teacher: "What are you talking about?"

Sandy: "Yesterday you said it was H to O!"

Teacher: "In this box I have a ten-foot snake."

Daniel: "You can't fool me . . . snakes don't have feet!"

13

SOCIAL STUDIES CLASS

Teacher: "Rick, where was the Declaration of Independence signed?"

Rick: "At the bottom!"

Teacher: "Gail, how long did the Hundred Years War last?"

Gail: "I don't know."

Teacher: "Think! How old is a six-year-old girl?"

Gail: "Six."

Teacher: "Well, then how long did the Hundred Years War last?"

Gail: "Six years!"

Teacher: "Class, close your geography books. Who can tell me where Mexico is?"
John: "I know—page 21."

Teacher: "Javier, go to the map and find North America."
Javier: "Here it is!"
Teacher: "Correct. Now class, who discovered North America?"
Class: "Javier!"

What's a snake's favorite subject?
Hiss-tory.

Social studies teacher: "Wendi, name the capital of every state."
Wendi: "Washington, D.C."

Why did the students eat the social studies quiz?

The teacher told them it was a "piece of cake."

Where is the English Channel?
I don't know. Our television set doesn't pick it up!

What is the most popular sentence at school?

"I don't know!"

Crystal: "Mom, I learned to write in school today!"

Mom: "What did you write?"

Crystal: "I don't know—I haven't learned to read yet!"

LANGUAGE ARTS CLASS

Teacher: "David, what comes after the letter 'O'?"

David: "Yeah!"

English teacher: "Tony, your spelling is terrible. Don't you ever read a dictionary?"

Tony: "No, I'll wait for the movie!"

Teacher: "Jennifer, give me a sentence starting with 'I'."

Jennifer: "I is ..."

Teacher: "No, Jennifer. Always say 'I am ...'."

Jennifer: "OK. I am the ninth letter of the alphabet!"

Teacher: "Steven, how do you spell crocodile?"

Steven: "K-R-O-K-O-D-I-A-L."

Teacher: "No Steven, that's wrong."

Steven: "Maybe it's wrong, but you asked me how I spell it!"

When is a yellow schoolbook not a yellow schoolbook?

When it is read!

English teacher: "What is an autobiography?"

Abe: "I know! I know! It's the life story of a car!"

What is better than a dog that can count?

A spelling bee.

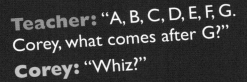

Teacher: "A, B, C, D, E, F, G. Corey, what comes after G?"

Corey: "Whiz?"

GRADES

Teacher: "Sam, you got a 'C' on your exam. What does that mean to you?"

Sam: "Congratulations."

Jimmy's mother: "Jimmy told me he got 100 on his tests yesterday!"

Counselor: "Yes, he did—a 50 in spelling and a 50 in arithmetic."

What marks did you get in physical education last semester?

I didn't get any marks, only bruises!

HOMEWORK

What did Patrick do when his puppy chewed up his dictionary?

He took the words right out of her mouth.

burp (burp) *n*., 1. a belch; eructation.

Juan: "Dad, can you please help me find the lowest common denominator in this problem?"

Dad: "Don't tell me they haven't found it yet! I remember looking for it way back when I was a boy!"

Teacher: "Naomi, did your parents help you with these homework problems?"

Naomi: "No, I got them all wrong by myself!"

19

GETTING THERE AND BACK

Makayla: "Dave, are you going to take the bus after school?"

Dave: "No. My mother would only make me take it back!"

Teacher: "Ross, you've been late to school every day since this semester began. What's the reason?"

Ross: "I can't help it. The sign on the street says, 'School Zone, Go Slow'."

Why didn't the flower go to school on its bike?

The petals were broken.

Principal: "Juan, you're late for school. Doesn't your watch tell you what time it is?"

Juan: "No—I have to look at it!"

Teacher: "Kathleen, why are you late for school?"

Kathleen: "I couldn't help it. School started before I got here."

Principal Howland: "Michael, you missed school yesterday, didn't you?"

Michael: "Not very much!"

Principal Howland: "Hannah, why were you late?"

Hannah: "Sorry, I overslept."

Principal: "You mean you need to sleep at home too?"

Dad: "Son, I hear you skipped school yesterday to play football!"

John: "No I didn't, and I have the fish to prove it!"

Principal Howland: "Why are you late this morning?"

Devin: "Because of the alarm clock. Everyone got up except for me."

Principal: "How was that?"

Devin: "There are eight of us in the family and the alarm was set for seven!"

Dad: "So son, how do you like going to school?"

Thomas: "The going is fine. So is the coming home. But I'm not too keen on the time in-between!"

Why can't you whisper in school?

It's not aloud!

THE RULES (AND BREAKING THEM)

PRINCIPAL

TGIF

Teacher: "This is the fifth time this week I've had to punish you. What do you have to say for yourself?"

Ron: "Thank goodness it's Friday!"

Isabelle: "Principal Howland said I could do anything I wanted for recess."

Chantal: "What did you do?"

Isabelle: "I went home!"

Teacher: "Brent, I told you to stand at the end of the line!"

Brent: "I tried, but there was someone already there!"

Teacher: "Danita, you aren't paying attention to me. Are you having trouble hearing?"

Danita: "No, I'm having trouble listening!"

Corey: "Teacher, would you ever be mad at me for something I didn't do?"

Teacher: "Of course not."

Corey: "That's good—I didn't do my homework!"

Teacher: "Tony, why are you running?"

Tony: "I'm running to stop a fight."

Teacher: "Between who?"

Tony: "Me and the kid who's chasing me!"

Teacher: "Alan, you know you can't sleep in my class."

Alan: "I know. But maybe if you were just a little quieter, I could!"

23

WRITING JOKES CAN BE AS MUCH FUN AS READING THEM!

Daffynitions are fun to write and even funnier to say. Daffynitions give a word a different kind of definition that usually makes a pun (a play on words) or funny comment.

There are some daffynitions on page 10. Here's one:

An Adder: The kind of snake that knows his numbers

An adder is a type of snake. But you could also say that someone who can add up numbers is an adder. We all know that snakes can't add up numbers and that is why this is funny.

Go back and re-read all the jokes in this book. Identify the jokes that are daffynitions. Which ones do you think are funny? Think about why you think they are funny.

YOU TRY IT!

Get together with some friends who also like jokes—or you can do this by yourself.

STEP 1: Go to the library and have each member of the group pick out a book on their favorite topic or subject (for example: math, snakes, knights, rocks). Look through the book for terms that you know could also mean something else. For example, if spelling is your favorite subject, you already have the makings of a daffynition! One meaning of **spell** is to list the letters that make up a word, but **spell** can also describe something a wizard might make. The daffynition is:

Spelling: A wizard's favorite subject

STEP 2: After everyone has a list of words, close the books and start brainstorming. Let everyone share their ideas for daffynitions using the words found in their books. Have one person write the ideas down. Don't say whether you think they are good or bad ideas, just get them all down on paper.

STEP 3: After all the daffynition ideas are down on paper, work as a group to decide which jokes work well. Have a member of the group read them out loud. Keep the ones everyone laughs at. Keep working on the ones that didn't get a laugh, or move on to a different subject. If you are working by yourself, read the jokes out loud to friends or family to see which ones they think are funny.

Don't stop here!

Collect your jokes and daffynitions in a journal and share with your family and friends when they need a good laugh!